Answers Academy

Biblical Apologetics for Real Life!

Participant's
Workbook

answersingenesis

Petersburg, Kentucky, USA

Answers Academy: Participant's Workbook

Third printing March 2010

For more information, write:
Answers in Genesis
2800 Bullittsburg Church Rd.
Petersburg, KY 41080

ISBN: 1893345-49-1

Text design by Diane King
Packaging and cover design by Brandie Lucas

Printed in the United States of America

TABLE OF CONTENTS

INTRODUCTION

OUR WESTERN WORLD is rapidly abandoning its biblical heritage. Almost daily, we see evidence that our nation is not as Christian as it once was: "gay marriage" is a hot topic, innocent people are murdered hourly in the name of "convenience" as abortion and "mercy killings" increase, and after every tragic event the question is asked, "How can there be a loving God in the midst of all this death and destruction?"

In the midst of this moral storm, many people are tossed to and fro, with many of them finally jumping ship, and eventually leaving the church. Increasingly faced with attacks by the world about the authority and accuracy of the Bible, they have found no answers to their questions. The "fact" of millions of years of earth history and evolution has shown them that the Bible's account of origins is wrong. So, they conclude, why trust its moral teachings?

This curriculum is designed to help reverse this tragic trend by showing that with what we know about science, anyone who thinks at all should believe the Bible *is* true when it comes to origins and its message of salvation still stands.

The aim of this course is to provide "biblical apologetics for real life" by enabling you to answer the questions the world is asking about the authority and accuracy of the Bible: What about natural selection? Don't radiometric dating methods prove the earth is millions of years old? Hasn't science proven there is no God?

During these thirteen lessons, you will discover *why* it is important to provide answers to skeptics and *how* to provide those answers with solid teaching on what the Bible says about biology, geology and astronomy. We'll show you that, contrary to popular belief, operational science actually *confirms* what the Bible teaches, but runs counter to evolutionary and "millions of years" ideas. By helping to rebuild the foundation of the Christian faith, *Answers Academy* enables us to understand our need for salvation and the biblical basis for morality. As you understand these vital answers, you, in turn, will be able to share with others who just don't know what to believe anymore.

Defending the Faith Part 1
Giving a Reasoned & Logical Defense of Christianity

Video Notes

- The origins of the universe as explained by those who don't believe God created life

"The cosmos is all that is or ever was or ever will be." (Carl Sagan, *Cosmos*, 1980, p. 4)

- The history of the universe as recorded in God's Word (Seven C's of History)

  Creation   no god

  Corruption   Big Bang

  Catastrophe

  Confusion

  Christ

  Cross

  Consummation

- The origin of death

- Same evidence, different interpretations

- Different pair of glasses: man decides truth vs. God's Word is Truth

- Present is key to past vs. revelation from someone who was there

- Science vs. religion issue

- Define observational science

- Define historical science

- Limitations of observational science

- Science confirms the Bible but doesn't prove it

Video Review Questions

1. Describe how a person with a naturalistic worldview (everything came about through chance and natural processes, with man determining truth) would explain the following. Then describe how a person with a biblical worldview (God created everything, as stated in His Word, and God determines truth) would explain them:

	Naturalistic Worldview	Biblical Worldview
Origin of the universe		
Origin of man		
Grand Canyon		
Dinosaurs		
Death		
Truth		

2. Let's return to the question we asked before the video—would you agree or disagree that creationists and evolutionists have the same evidence? Has your answer changed? Why or why not?

3. List and describe the major events of history as covered by the Seven C's of History.

4. Explain why, biblically, the earth cannot be millions of years old.

5. Explain why we see death and suffering in the world today.

6. Do fossils exist in the past or present? Explain your answer.

7. Describe the differences between observational (operational) and historical (origins) science.

8. What are some of the limitations of observable science in regard to interpreting the past?

9. What does Job 38:4 say about the past?

People to Know

CHARLES DARWIN (1809–1882)

While Charles Darwin did not invent the concept of evolution, he did popularize the idea of "molecules-to-man" evolution. His famous book *On the Origin of Species* was published in 1859. Darwin rejected Christianity after his young daughter, Annie, died. He was also greatly influenced by the works of geologist Sir Charles Lyell, who promoted the uniformitarian view of layers in geology. The major areas of Darwin's work include the struggle for existence, variation, natural selection and sexual selection.

SIR CHARLES LYELL (1797–1875)

A lawyer with a keen interest in geology, Lyell wrote the three-volume work *Principles of Geology*. This influential compilation promoted the uniformitarian view of geology, which states that only present-day processes at present-day rates of intensity should be used to interpret the rock record of past geological activity. He believed that layers of rock are formed by the slow accumulation of sediment over eons of time. Lyell's view of geology was taken up by Darwin and applied to biology.

CARL SAGAN (1934–1996)

An ardent evolutionist and atheist, Carl Sagan, Professor of Astronomy and Space Science at Cornell University, was an astronomer and author who achieved fame by popularizing science through books, magazines and the television series *Cosmos*. His 1985 novel *Contact* was the basis for the popular movie by the same name.

Life Application

Let's consider how we can apply the things we've learned today to our lives.

Think about those with whom you come in contact every day: family, friends, teachers, other students, etc. Think of one person with whom you would like to share your Christian faith. Write down that person's name and consider the view that person may have on each topic.

Then consider what information you would discuss with that person to counter that view, if it's not consistent with a biblical worldview.

Name _____

Topic	Naturalistic View	Biblical View	Material to Share
Origin of the universe			
Origin of man			
Grand Canyon			
Age of the earth			
Dinosaurs			
Death before sin			
Moral authority (truth)			

For Next Week

For the next lesson, please read and meditate on these verses in preparation for the second part on defending the faith.

- 1 Peter 3:15
- Romans 1:20

Optional Activity

(This will be assigned at your teacher's discretion.)

At the beginning of this study (as early in the study as possible) conduct a survey, using some of the following questions, to find out what beliefs people have about the following topics:

- Do you think the Bible is relevant today?

- Do you think the Bible's history, like the account of Noah's Flood, is true?

- How do you think the universe came into existence?

- How do you think man came into existence?

- Do you think science disproves the Bible?

- Do you think dinosaurs lived at the same time as man?

- Who determines right and wrong?

- Do you believe in absolute authority?

- Who determines absolute authority?

Glossary of Terms

The following terms are discussed in this lesson:

HISTORICAL SCIENCE (ALSO CALLED *ORIGINS SCIENCE*)

Science that deals with past events—unique, unrepeatable, unobservable events. You can't test events that happened in the past.

NATURALISM

Naturalism is the belief that only natural processes are permitted as explanations for the origin of life. This view excludes any miraculous creative action (intelligence)—even if such an explanation best fits the facts. Naturalism is the deliberate rejection of God's Word and its authority in relation to the history of the world.

OBSERVATIONAL SCIENCE (ALSO CALLED *OPERATIONAL SCIENCE*)

Science that deals with the way the present world works, and generally concerns things that we can observe and repeatedly test. For example, we can consistently get the same undisputed temperature for the boiling point of water since we can observe and repeat the test conditions.

PRESUPPOSITION

The action or an act of presupposing; a supposition antecedent to knowledge; the assumption of the existence or truth of something, as a preliminary to action, argument, etc.

DEFENDING THE FAITH PART 2
Giving a Reasoned & Logical Defense of Christianity

Video Notes

- Observational science can't prove the Bible scientifically, but it confirms the Bible's history.

- The Human Genome Project confirms that there's only one race—the human race.

- God's Word gives us the right starting point. The Bible's history makes sense of the fossils, people groups, DNA, variations in dogs, Grand Canyon's rock layers, etc.

- All facts are interpreted—there's no such thing as a neutral fact.

- When receiving news through the media, we are getting interpretations of events or subjects based on the news reporter's starting points.

- A person's starting point determines how he or she understands the meaning of life and morality, in addition to things like geology, biology, astronomy, etc.

- God's Word gives us a basis for right and wrong.

- Many people have been brainwashed into thinking that observational science has disproved the Bible and that the Bible is an outdated religious book.

Video Review Questions

1. Discuss how observational science confirms the Bible's history through the following:

   Fossils

   Different people groups

DNA

Animal kinds

Grand Canyon

2. In what ways have people been brainwashed into believing the Bible is not true?

3. What has contributed to the collapse of Christian morality in our culture today?

4. Explain the meaning of the statement, "Facts are meaningless."

DID YOU KNOW?

The government-funded Natural History Museum and the Science Center in London have displays that declare things such as the following:

*   The Flood of Noah is a myth.
*   The world is 4.5 billion years old.
*   Evolution is a fact.
*   Dinosaurs evolved into birds—there is absolutely no doubt.
*   Humans are not special—basically, we are no different from a chimpanzee or a fruit fly, and their genes are much the same as ours.

5. Explain how religion remains in public schools even though the Bible and Christianity were thrown out of public schools years ago.

6. Explain how an atheist can determine what is evil and what is good.

7. Describe how questions, such as, "What's missing?" can influence a person's interpretation of evidence, such as in the case of the circle that was missing its sides.

8. Look up Romans 1:20 and discuss what it means.

9. Explain the connection between evolutionary ideas and abortion.

People to Know

JAMES ALLAN

Dr. James Allan is a retired senior lecturer in the department of genetics at the University of Stellenbosch, South Africa. He has researched the genetics of fruit flies, snails, chickens, dairy cattle and fish. Read about his dramatic change from a belief in evolution to a belief that God created everything in six days, 6,000 years ago. It's online at www.Answers InGenesis.org/Allan.

Life Application

Let's consider how we can apply the things we've learned today to our lives.

When analyzing information or sharing our faith with someone, it's important to know that person's starting point or worldview. Think about the following people and write down what their worldview is. Consider how their worldview expresses itself (what they say and do, decisions they make, etc.).

	Worldview
Your parents	
Your local newspaper editor	
Your favorite actor/actress	
Your favorite athlete	
Your pastor	
The characters in the last movie you watched	

For Next Week

For the next lesson, please read and meditate on these verses before we look at how to answer the question, "Where did God come from?"

- Genesis 1:1
- Romans 1:20
- 1 Peter 3:15
- 2 Timothy 2:24–26
- 2 Peter 3:5
- Jeremiah 17:9
- 2 Corinthians 4:4

Optional Activity

(This will be assigned at your teacher's discretion.)

Choose a news topic (such as dinosaurs) and find articles that approach the topic from different perspectives (biblical and naturalistic). Analyze the differences among the reports and separate the actual facts from the interpretation of the facts.

One example would be the March 2005 discovery (by Mary Higby Schweitzer of North Carolina State University) of blood cells, soft tissue and complete blood vessels in a *Tyrannosaurus rex* leg bone.

Pick sources that represent each worldview. Possible sources include *Time* magazine, *World* magazine, AnswersinGenesis.org, MSNBC.com and the *New York Times*.

Glossary of Terms

The following term is discussed in this lesson:

AXIOM

That which is thought worthy or fit, that which commends itself as self-evident; to hold worthy. A proposition that commends itself to general acceptance; a well-established or universally conceded principle; a maxim, rule, law.

WHERE DID GOD COME FROM?
The All-Important Question

Video Notes

- Different ways to interpret evidence.

- Design implies a designer.

- The science of information theory confirms God is the Creator.

- Words are meaningless without a code.

- Blind faith—who has it?

- Observational science—what does it prove?

- The Bible's history is true—the history as told in Genesis 1–11 is foundational to the rest of the Bible.

- It is important to give a logical, reasoned defense of the Christian faith.

Video Review Questions

1. Now that you've seen the video, how would you respond to the question, "Who made God?"

2. A common Christian argument for God is that the marvelous design of animals and plants implies a designer. Even ardent atheists agree that design is evident in nature. Explain the argument that evolutionists use to counter this point.

3. Describe how the science of information theory confirms a Creator God.

Beads on a rope

DNA

4. Dr. Werner Gitt has stated that, in real science, "matter never produces information." Complete the following sentence:

Codes never arise from _____ by themselves, and

codes always come from an _____.

5. What was Dr. Richard Dawkins' response when asked to give an example of new information being produced from matter and added into the genome?

6. Describe what it means to have blind faith. What are some examples of people having blind faith?

7. In what ways can a Christian appear to have blind faith?

8. Read 1 Peter 3:15 and 2 Timothy 2:24–26. What do these verses teach about the need to provide accurate answers to those who ask questions about our faith?

People to Know

FRANCIS CRICK (1916–2004) AND JAMES WATSON (1928–)

Crick and Watson's description of DNA's double-helix structure opened the door to the eventual sequencing of the human genome. Crick and Watson (along with Maurice Wilkins) were awarded the Nobel Prize in 1962 for their discovery. By breaking down the functions of life in terms of chemistry and physics, these ardent atheists hoped to show that natural processes—not a Creator—produced life.

RICHARD DAWKINS

An ardent atheist and evolutionary biologist, Dawkins has authored many books against creation, such as *The Blind Watchmaker*. A popular international spokesman for Darwinian evolution, he was awarded Oxford University's chair as Professor of the Public Understanding of Science. In 1996, Dawkins, who has frequently referred to himself as the "Devil's disciple," was awarded the Humanist of the Year award for his work.

WERNER GITT

A respected information scientist, Dr. Gitt served for many years as a director and professor at the German Federal Institute of Physics and

DID YOU KNOW?

The genetic code is not an outcome of raw chemistry but of elaborate decoding machinery in the ribosome (the "protein factory" of cells). This decoding machinery is itself encoded in the DNA. The noted philosopher of science Sir Karl Popper pointed out:

"Thus the code cannot be translated except by using certain products of its translation. This constitutes a baffling circle; a really vicious circle, it seems, for any attempt to form a model or theory of the genesis of the genetic code."

So, such a system must be fully in place before it could work at all—a property called irreducible complexity. This means that it is impossible to be built by natural selection working on small changes.

Technology (Physikalisch-Technische Bundesanstalt, Braunschweig) and as head of the department of information technology. He has authored a number of popular creation books, including *In the Beginning Was Information.*

Life Application

Let's consider how we can apply the things we've learned today to our lives.

When sharing or defending your faith with another person, it's important to know how the other person thinks and what kind of biases and presuppositions they may have. Think about how you might share your faith with others using what you've learned in this lesson. How will you approach the following people with this new information?

Friends:

Family:

Teachers:

Skeptics:

Non-Christian acquaintances:

For Next Week

Please read and meditate on these verses in preparation for the next lesson:

* Genesis 1:1–31

Optional Activity

(This will be assigned at your teacher's discretion.)

The Bible gives several reasons that people don't believe in God. Look up the following verses and explain the reasons given in each verse.

• 2 Peter 3:5

• Jeremiah 17:9

• 2 Corinthians 4:4

Glossary of Terms

The following terms are discussed in this lesson:

APOLOGETICS

The Greek term comes from a word meaning "out of logic/reason." It refers to a reasoned defense that would be given in a court of law. The classic example is Plato's *Apology*, Socrates' defense against the charges of atheism and corrupting the youth.

OPERATIONAL SCIENCE

Operational science (also called *observational science*) deals with the way the present world works and generally concerns things that we can observe and repeatedly test. For example, we can consistently get the same undisputed temperature for the boiling point of water since we can observe and repeat the test conditions.

ORIGINS SCIENCE

Origins science (also called *historical science*) deals with how we apply observations made in the present to unobservable events in the past. Scientific observations must be *interpreted* when applied to past events.

PRESUPPOSITION

The action or an act of presupposing; a supposition antecedent to knowledge; the assumption of the existence or truth of something, as a preliminary to action, argument, etc.

4

AFTER ITS KIND PART 1
The Truth about Natural Selection

Video Notes

* Biblical view of biology

"The origin of domestic dog from wolves has been established ... . We examined the mitochondrial DNA (mtDNA) sequence variation among 654 domestic dogs representing all major dog populations worldwide ... suggesting a common origin from a single gene pool for all dog populations." (Savolainen, et al., "Genetic Evidence for an East Asian Origin of Domestic Dogs," *Science* 298(5598):1610-1613, November 22, 2002)

"Two-kilogram teacup poodles; 90-kg mastiffs; slender greyhounds; squat English bulldogs: for a single species, canines come in a vast array of shapes and sizes. Even more remarkably, they all come from the same stock ... . Only subtle differences distinguish dogs from coyotes, jackals, and other canids, making family trees difficult to construct and the timing of the transition from wolf to dog hard to pinpoint." (Elizabeth Pennisi, "Canine Evolution: A Shaggy Dog History," *Science* 298(5598):1540-1542, November 22, 2002)

* The nature of natural selection

* Claim: Creationists believe that God created all living things in exactly the form that we see them today

- Problems with the standard "design" arguments

- The large amount of variability in genes (e.g., between two people)

Video Review Questions

1. Read Genesis 1:1–31. Identify the number of times the text uses the phrases "after its kind," "after their kind," etc.

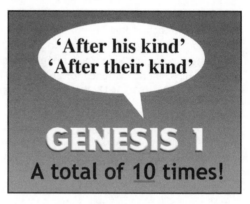

2. Return to the question asked before the video, "Do you agree that natural selection and molecules-to-man evolution are basically the same processes?" Has your answer changed? Why or why not?

3. Now that you've seen the video, would you agree or disagree with the statement, "God created all living things in exactly the form we see them today"? Why or why not?

4. How many different genetic combinations are possible from the union of one man and one woman?

5. Summarize a major problem with the standard "design" argument.

6. Fill out the "disciplines" chart. Take a few minutes to think about which aspects of biology fall under "operational science" and which fall under "origins science."

DISCIPLINE: BIOLOGY	OPERATIONAL SCIENCE	ORIGINS SCIENCE
	Dissecting animals	

Arguments Creationists Should NOT Use

Following is an argument that some people have used to explain the difference between natural selection and particles-to-people evolution. It is, however, not recommended because it doesn't effectively deal with the root of the problem. For a more extensive list of out-of-date arguments, see www.AnswersInGenesis.org/dont_use.

- **"Creationists believe in microevolution but not macroevolution."** These terms, which focus on "small" vs. "large" changes, detract from the key issue of information. That is, particles-to-people evolution requires changes that increase genetic information, but the only thing that we observe is sorting and loss of information. We have yet to see even a "micro" increase in information, although such changes should be frequent if evolution were true. Conversely, we do observe "macro" changes that involve no new information (e.g., when a control gene is switched on or off). See www.Answers InGenesis.org/train for additional information.

People to Know

EDWARD BLYTH (1810–1873)

Edward Blyth was a creationist who discussed natural selection 25 years *before* Darwin!

DID YOU KNOW?

The peppered moths are often touted today in many textbooks as proof-positive of "evolution in action." Even though this would be nothing more than natural selection and thus not a problem for creationists, recent information has revealed that the whole peppered moth scenario was faked!

- The famous photos of light and dark moths resting on a lichen-covered tree trunk were *faked* by pinning and/or gluing dead moths onto logs or trunks.

- The filmed "experiments" involved either dead moths or laboratory moths (so stuporous they had to be warmed up first) that were manually placed on tree trunks in the daytime.

For more information, see www.AnswersInGenesis.org/moths.

WALTER VEITH

Dr. Walter J. Veith, BSc (Hons), MSc (cum laude), PhD, is a full professor at the University of the Western Cape (Republic of South Africa), where he holds the chair of zoology.

Life Application

Let's consider how we can apply the things we've learned today to our lives.

If you saw a picture on a calendar that looked like this, what should your reaction be?

WITH THEIR KEEN EYESIGHT AND POWERFUL TALONS, EAGLES ARE BEAUTIFULLY DESIGNED TO CAPTURE AND KILL THEIR PREY.

For Next Week

For next week, please read and meditate on these verses in preparation for next week's lesson on natural selection:

- Jeremiah 17:9
- 2 Peter 3:5–6
- Genesis 3:20; 4:1–2, 25; 5:3–4

Optional Activities

(These will be assigned at your teacher's discretion.)

1. Write a research paper about Edward Blyth.

2. Research the credentials and careers of present-day creationist biologists, such as David DeWitt, Pierre Jerlstrom and Lane Lester. What types of degrees did they receive? From what schools? What are they doing now? What types of careers are open to Christians interested in studying biology? See www.AnswersInGenesis.org/bios for help.

Glossary of Terms

The following terms are mentioned in this lesson:

CREATED "KIND"

From Genesis 1, the ability to produce offspring (that is, to breed with one another) seems to define the original created kinds. One possible way to determine an original created "kind" is if two animals or two plants can mate and produce a truly fertilized egg, then they probably belong to (i.e., are descended from) the same original created kind. If these animals or plants are from different genera in a family, it suggests that the whole family might have come from one created kind. If the genera are in different families within an order, it suggests that the whole order may have derived from the original created kind. On the other hand, if two species will not hybridize, it does not necessarily prove that they are not originally from the same kind.

For more information, see www.AnswersInGenesis.org/liger.

DOMINANT GENES

An allele or trait that is expressed when paired with a recessive allele.

RECESSIVE GENE

An allele or trait that is not expressed when paired with a dominant allele.

SPECIATION

The formation of a reproductively isolated group that generally has certain characteristics which distinguish it from other members of the same species. For more information, see www.AnswersIn Genesis.org/speciation.

AFTER ITS KIND PART 2
The Truth about Natural Selection

Video Notes

- Dispersion after the Flood

"All point mutations that have been studied on the molecular level turn out to reduce the genetic information and not to increase it." (Lee Spetner, *Not by Chance*, p. 138, 1997)

- How the Ice Age aided dispersion

- The development of a new species

- The human "race" issue

- How mutations function

- Antibiotic resistance

- Noah's Ark and all those animals

- Fast population growth

"Elephants unlimited. During their lifetime, a pair of elephants could give rise to 60 descendants, more than enough to replace the original pair. At this rate, their family could swell to 19 million living members after 700 years!" (Sign in the Darwin exhibit at the British Museum of Natural History)

- Speciation today

"A study in the latest *Science* shows that natural selection can reshape organisms faster than even some diehard evolutionists might have predicted." (*US News and World Report*, January 24, 2000, p. 49)

"He and his colleagues saw an increase in wing size … . And they saw the same increase in the fruit flies from North America, even though the species had spent only a brief time on the continent. Indeed, Andrew Hendry of the University of Massachusetts, Amherst, who has recently completed a survey of evolutionary rates, says that the change 'is as fast as I have ever seen … . I think this will shake up a lot of people.'

"Schluter's team found that the sticklebacks they studied represent an even more dramatic case of parallel evolution … and [their finding] shows that natural selection can yield new species.

"The more researchers probe the corners of nature's laboratory, the more evidence they are likely to find supporting the importance of natural selection, Mitton says. For example, he sees repeated patterns of evolution in some traits of the pinyon pines that he studies. These examples 'say that natural selection can cause a population to change very quickly and hint that speciation could [occur] very quickly,' he notes." (Elizabeth Pennisi, "Nature Steers a Predictable Course," *Science* 287(5451):207–209, January 2000)

- Why do people reject the biblical view?

"Our willingness to accept scientific claims that are against common sense is the key to an understanding of the real struggle between science and the supernatural. We take the side of science *in spite* of the patent absurdity of some of its constructs, *in spite* of its failure to fulfill many of its extravagant promises of health and life, *in spite* of the tolerance of the scientific community for unsubstantiated just-so stories, because we have a prior commitment, a commitment to materialism.

"It is not that the methods and institutions of science somehow compel us to accept a material explanation of the phenomenal world, but, on the contrary, that we are forced by our *a priori* adherence to material causes to create an apparatus of investigation and a set of concepts that produce material explanations, no matter how counter-intuitive, no matter how mystifying to the uninitiated. Moreover, that materialism is an absolute, for we cannot allow a Divine Foot in the door." (Richard Lewontin, "Billions and Billions of Demons," *New York Review*, January 9, 1997, p. 31)

- Mars Flood

- Conclusion

Video Review Questions

1. Let's return to the kangaroo question. After watching the video, has your answer about kangaroos living in the Middle East changed?

2. Explain why the 13 species of "Darwin's finches" confirm the biblical view of variation within kinds rather than showing "evolution in action."

3. Describe your understanding of how natural selection operates within a biblical framework.

4. Read Jeremiah 17:9 and 2 Peter 3:5–6. What do these verses teach about why people don't accept the fact that observational science confirms the Bible?

5. Fill out the "disciplines" chart. Take a few minutes to think about which aspects of genetics (the scientific study of DNA, etc.) fall under "operational" science and which fall under "origins" science.

DISCIPLINE: GENETICS	OPERATIONAL SCIENCE	ORIGINS SCIENCE

Arguments Creationists Should NOT Use

Following are two arguments that some creationists have used when dealing with the topic of natural selection. But these arguments have serious errors. See www.AnswersInGenesis.org/dont_use for a more extensive list of arguments creationists shouldn't use.

- **"There are no beneficial mutations."** This is not true, since some changes *do* confer an advantage in some situations. Rather, we should say, "We have yet to find a mutation that *increases genetic information*, even in those rare instances where the mutation confers an advantage." For examples of information *loss* that is advantageous, see www. AnswersInGenesis.org/beetle.

- **"No new species have been produced."** This is not true. New species have been observed to form. In fact, *rapid* speciation is an important part of the creation model. But this speciation is within the "kind" and involves no new genetic information. See www. AnswersInGenesis.org/speciation.

DID YOU KNOW?

Many skeptics have claimed that for Cain to find a wife, there must have been other "races" of people on earth who were not descendants of Adam and Eve.

However ...

We read in 1 Corinthians 15:45 that Adam was "the first man." God did not start by making a whole group of men. Genesis 3:20 states, "Adam called his wife's name Eve; because she was the mother of all living." So Adam was the first man, and Eve was the first woman.

Cain was the first child of Adam and Eve recorded in Scripture (Genesis 4:1), followed by Abel (Genesis 4:2) and Seth (Genesis 4:25). Even though only these three males are mentioned by name, Adam and Eve had other children. Genesis 5:4 sums up the life of Adam and Eve: "And the days of Adam after he had fathered Seth were eight hundred years. And he fathered sons and daughters." This does not say *when* they were born. Many could have been born in the 130 years (Genesis 5:3) before Seth was born.

If we now work totally from Scripture, without any personal prejudices or extrabiblical ideas, then back at the beginning, during the first generation, brothers had to marry sisters; otherwise, there would have been no more generations!

We are not told when Cain married or any details about the other marriages and children, but we can say for certain that some brothers had to marry their sisters at the beginning of human history. Note that this was before the law of Moses forbade such practices; Abraham married his half-sister, Sarah, without violating this law, which was decreed centuries later.

For more information, including the scientific reason that there would not have been deformities from such close intermarriages in early human history, visit www.AnswersInGenesis.org/cains_wife.

People to Know

RICHARD LEWONTIN

Professor Richard Lewontin, a geneticist (and self-proclaimed Marxist), is a renowned champion of neo-Darwinism and certainly one of the world's leaders in evolutionary biology. See his quote at www.Answers InGenesis.org/lewontin.

CAROLUS LINNAEUS (1707–1778)

Linnaeus, the founder of the science of taxonomy, tried to determine the created kinds. He opposed the pre-Darwin evolutionary ideas of his day, pointing out that life was not a continuum, or a "great chain of being," as taught by the ancient pagan Greeks. He defined a "species" as a group of organisms that could interbreed among themselves but not with other groups, akin to the Genesis concept. In his mature years he did extensive hybridization (crossbreeding) experiments and realized that his "species" concept was too narrow for the species to be considered created kinds; he thought that the genus perhaps corresponded better with the created kind.

Today, most creationists agree that if two animals or two plants can mate and produce a truly fertilized egg, then they probably belong to (i.e., have descended from) the same original created kind.

LEE SPETNER

With a PhD in physics from MIT, Dr. Spetner taught information and communication theory for years at Johns Hopkins University. In 1962 he accepted a fellowship in biophysics at that institution, where he worked on solving problems in signal/noise relationships in DNA electron micrographs. His book *Not by Chance!* aims a deathblow at the heart of the whole neo-Darwinian story. Find a review of his book at www.AnswersinGenesis.org/spetner.

Life Application

Let's consider how we can apply the things we've learned today to our lives.

1. Imagine you were reading your local newspaper and you came across a "letter to the editor" that claimed, "Bacteria evolve resistance to antibiotics all the time—that proves evolution happens!" How would you respond?

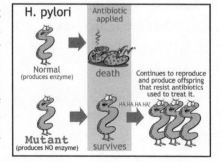

2. One way skeptics enjoy attacking the Bible is with the question, "How could Noah fit all the animals on the Ark?" How would you reply to this question?

For Next Week

For next week, please read and meditate on these verses in preparation for next week's lesson on natural selection:

- Genesis 1:9–10
- Genesis 6:11–8:14
- Genesis 1:14

Optional Activities

(These will be assigned at your teacher's discretion.)

1. Write a research paper on the life and work of Carolus Linnaeus.

2. Research the credentials and work of various creationist geneticists, such as James Allen, Andre Eggen, or Georgia Purdom. Where did they study? What did they study? What is their current occupation? What careers are available in the field of genetics? See www. AnswersInGenesis.org/bios for help.

Glossary of Terms

The following terms are discussed in this lesson:

ADAPTATION

Changes within a population that allow it to become better suited to its environment.

ARTIFICIAL SELECTION

Human-directed process of selecting certain desired traits within a population.

DOMINANT GENES

An allele or trait that is expressed when paired with a recessive allele.

RECESSIVE GENES

An allele or trait that is not expressed when paired with a dominant allele.

6

THE ROCKS CRY OUT PART 1
The Earth Is Young!

Video Notes

*   Review of starting points

*   Brief history of geology
    Biblical view

    Catastrophic view

    Uniformitarian view

"My excuse for this lengthy and amateur digression into history is that I have been trying to show how I think geology got into the hands of the theoreticians who were conditioned by the social and political history of their day more than by observations in the field. ... In other words, we have allowed ourselves to be brain-washed into avoiding any interpretation of the past that involves extreme and what might be termed 'catastrophic' processes." (Derek Ager, *The Nature of the Stratigraphical Record,* Macmillan, London, pp. 46-47, 1981)

Regarding "Sutton Stone," a conglomerate dated as "Early Jurassic" (180–206 mya) near Swansea, England:

"This has usually been interpreted as the basal conglomerate of a diachronous transgressive sea. It has been suggested, with very little fossil evidence, that this conglomerate spans three to five ammonite zones and therefore up to five million years in time. I think it was deposited in a matter of hours or minutes." (Derek Ager, *The New Catastrophism,* Cambridge University Press, p. 120, 1993)

"Perhaps I am becoming a cynic in my old age, but I cannot help thinking that people find things that they expect to find. As Sir Edward Bailey (1953) said, 'to find a thing you have to believe it to be possible.'" (Derek Ager, *The New Catastrophism,* Cambridge University Press, pp. 190-191, 1993)

- How long does it take to form and erode rocks?

- Magic in the marsh

"Without any regard to the laws of geology, mud on the marsh is hardening into stone in a few years rather than the thousands it usually takes. ... Professor Coleman said the rock was forming faster than anybody had ever believed possible, with one stone creating itself in just six months. ... They often contain beautifully preserved fossils, where the detail of the soft flesh of the creature is caught as well as the bone, as it had no time to rot before the rock formed around it." (*Eastern Daily Press* [Norfolk, UK], Oct. 5, 1994, p. 7)

- The Scablands

"The 'establishment,' as represented by the United States Geological Society, closed ranks in opposition ... . Instead of testing Bretz's flood on its own merits, they rejected it on general principles. ... Bretz stood against a firm, highly restrictive dogma that never had made any sense: the emperor had been naked for a century. Charles Lyell, the godfather of geologic gradualism, had pulled a fast one in establishing the doctrine of imperceptible change." (Stephen Jay Gould, "The Great Scablands Debate," *Natural History* 87(7):12, 14, Aug.–Sept. 1978)

- Canyon Lakes Spillway

- Evidence of rapid successive deposition of sediments

    Lack of erosional features

    Soft sediment deformation of rocks

    Lack of bioturbation at interface between various layers

    Ripple marks, animal tracks, raindrops

    Polystrate fossils

    Fossil graveyards

- Review of how one's starting points influence how one interprets the facts

Video Review Questions

1. How has the information in this video influenced your beliefs about the time it takes for rocks to form?

2. How has this video changed your view of the relationship between the Bible and geology?

3. What influenced the uniformitarians more than actual observations of the rocks?

4. Fill out the "disciplines" chart. Take a few minutes to think about which aspects of geology fall under "operational" science and which fall under "origins" science.

DISCIPLINE: GEOLOGY	OPERATIONAL SCIENCE	ORIGINS SCIENCE

5. Begin to think about what Genesis 1:9–10 and Genesis 6:11–8:14 indicate about formation of the various rock layers we see today. We'll explore these passages in more detail in the next lesson.

Arguments Creationists Should NOT Use

When sharing with those who don't believe the Bible, make sure your arguments are up-to-date. Faulty arguments can ruin the credibility of creationists. (For this reason it is important to stay current by reading sound creationist literature.)

Following are a few arguments that should no longer be used because they are out-of-date, questionable or faulty.

For a more extensive list, see www.AnswersInGenesis.org/dont_use.

- **"Earth's axis was vertical before the Flood."** There is no basis for this claim. Seasons are mentioned in Genesis 1:14 *before* the Flood, which strongly suggests an axial tilt from the beginning. Some creationists believe that a change in axial tilt (but not from the vertical) started Noah's Flood. But a lot more evidence is needed, and this idea should be regarded as speculative, at least for now. Furthermore, computer modeling suggests that an upright axis would make temperature

DID YOU KNOW?

Have opals have been made in a laboratory in a matter of weeks?

Dr. Len Cramer, a Bible-believing Christian and Australian scientist who earned his Ph.D. in opal research, has discovered the secret (using operational science) that has enabled him to actually "grow" opals in glass jars stored in his wooden shed laboratory, and the process takes only a matter of weeks! Len's man-made opals are so good that even experienced Lightning Ridge miners can't tell the difference between them and opals found in the ground. Furthermore, scientists from Australia's CSIRO (Commonwealth Scientific and Industrial Research Organization) can't distinguish Len's opal from natural opal even under an electron microscope—they look identical!

Contrary to popular opinion, opals don't need millions of years to form—just the right conditions!

Visit www.AnswersInGenesis.org/opals for more information.

differences between the poles and equator far *more* extreme than now, while the current tilt of 23.5° is ideal. The moon has an important function in stabilizing this tilt; it appears to be perfectly designed, with a large relative size and an orbital plane close to the earth's (unlike most moons in our solar system).

- **Canopy theory** (the belief that there was a vapor covering [or canopy] around the earth between the time of creation and the Flood). This is not a direct teaching of Scripture, so there is no place for dogmatism. Also, no suitable scientific model has been developed that enables the atmosphere to hold sufficient water molecules and to avoid a "greenhouse effect" that would make the surface temperature intolerable for life. But some other creationists suggest a partial canopy. For more information on problems with the canopy idea, see www.AnswersInGenesis.org/flood_waters.

- **"Woolly mammoths were snap-frozen during the Flood catastrophe."** This claim contradicts the geological setting in which mammoths are found. It's most likely that they perished toward the end of the Ice Age, possibly in catastrophic dust storms. Partially digested stomach contents are not proof of a snap freeze because the elephant's stomach functions as a holding area—a mastodon was found in midwestern USA, where the ground is not frozen, with preserved stomach contents. See www.AnswersInGenesis.org/mam moth.

People to Know

DEREK AGER

One of the leading neo-catastrophists of the 1970s and 1980s was Derek Ager, a British evolutionary geologist and pantheist who had conducted geological investigations in about 50 countries of the world.

JOHN BAUMGARDNER

John Baumgardner, PhD (UCLA), who served for many years as a research scientist at the Los Alamos National Laboratory in New Mexico, is a geophysics professor at the Institute for Creation Research. His research has focused on detailed computer modeling of the structure and processes of the earth's interior, as well as a variety of other fluid dynamics phenomena.

J HARLAN BRETZ (1882–1981)

Observing the strange landforms of the Scablands in eastern Washington, the evolutionary geologist J Harlan Bretz postulated a flood of enormous magnitude to explain the formation of the landforms in that area. See www.AnswersInGenesis.org/missoula.

GEORGES CUVIER (1768–1832)

The Frenchman Georges Cuvier, a comparative anatomist and paleontologist, published his popular catastrophist *Theory of the Earth* in 1812. After studying fossils found primarily in the Paris Basin, he concluded that, over the course of untold ages, the area had endured many regional or nearly global catastrophic floods, the last of which was probably about 5,000 years ago. Cuvier apparently believed that God, after each catastrophe, supernaturally created new forms of life.

STEPHEN J. GOULD (1941–2002)

Perhaps the world's leading advocate of evolution until his death in 2002, atheist Stephen J. Gould was the author of many books and a professor of geology and paleontology at Harvard University.

CHARLES LYELL (1797–1875)

Charles Lyell, a trained lawyer who became a geologist, began publishing his three-volume *Principles of Geology* in 1830. Building on uniformitarian ideas, Lyell insisted that the geological features of the earth can, and indeed must, be explained by slow and gradual processes of erosion, sedimentation, earthquakes and volcanism operating at essentially the same rate, frequency and power as we observe today. He rejected any notion of regional or global catastrophism; earthquakes, volcanoes and floods in the past were no more frequent or powerful (on average) than those in the present. By the 1840s, his view became the ruling paradigm in geology. See www.AnswersInGenesis.org/niagara.

Life Application

Let's consider how we can apply the things we've learned today to our lives.

The "millions of years" story is all around us—museums, national parks, television, movies. Sometimes the pervasiveness of the story can seem overwhelming. The next time you see a sign or video that shouts "millions of years," take a minute to see if you can distinguish between the actual facts and the *interpretations* imposed on the facts.

For example, take a look at this sign from Grand Canyon:

GRAND CANYON

Time: Although rocks exposed in the canyon are hundreds of millions of years old, geologists estimate an age of six million years or less for the canyon itself.

*Text taken from an interpretive sign in the Grand Canyon.

Analyze the news reports given to you by your teacher. Which statements are facts. Which are interpretations?

For Next Week

For the next lesson, please read and meditate on these chapters of the Bible in preparation for the lesson:

- Genesis 6–9

Optional Activities

(These will be assigned at your teacher's discretion.)

1. Research the various "Scriptural geologists." Choose one and write a report about him. See www.AnswersInGenesis.org/geologists or Dr. Mortenson's book *The Great Turning Point*.

2. Research and write a report on various evidences that confirm the biblical record of the Flood.

Glossary of Terms

The following terms are discussed in this lesson:

AMMONITE
Ocean-dwelling shell animal

BIOTURBATION
Disturbance (burrowing, cracking, etc.) of the surface of land or the ocean floor by plants or animal activity.

CATASTROPHISM
The idea that the earth has suffered many regional or global catastrophes over the course of millions of years, which produced the fossil record.

DIACHRONOUS TRANSGRESSIVE SEA
A sea that has covered the land multiple times during the past.

DOGMA
An authoritative principle, belief or statement of ideas or opinion, especially one considered to be absolutely true.

OBSERVATIONAL (EMPIRICAL) SCIENCE
Science that deals with repeatable, observable processes in the present.

POLYSTRATE FOSSILS
Fossils (usually trees) that cut through several rock layers.

UNIFORMITARIANISM
The idea that all geologic phenomena may be explained as the result of existing forces operating uniformly since the origin of the earth to the present time.

7

THE ROCKS CRY OUT PART 2
The Earth Is Young!

Video Notes

- Reasons the Flood was global

- Purpose of the Flood

- Nature of the Flood

- Depth of the Flood

- Duration of the Flood

- Expected results of the Flood

- Overview of the biblical geologic model

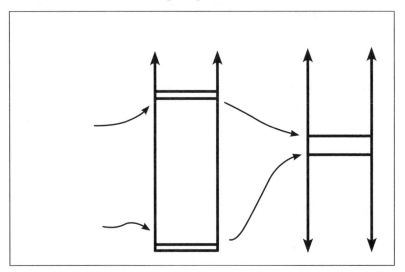

- Different physical processes used to gauge the age of the earth

- Sea salt

- Erosion of continents

- Helium in the atmosphere

- Cave formation

"From 1924 to 1988, there was a visitor's sign above the entrance to Carlsbad Caverns that said Carlsbad was at least 260 million years old. In 1988, the sign was changed to read 7 to 10 million years old. Then, for a little while, the sign read that it was 2 million years old. Now the sign is gone." (Jerry Trout [cave specialist with the Forest Service], "Descent," *Arizona Highways*, Jan. 1993, pp. 10-11)

- Living fossils

- Time required to form fossils

"Fossilization is a process that can take anything from a few hours to millions of years. ... The amount of time that it takes for a bone to become completely permineralized is highly variable. If the groundwater is heavily laden with minerals in solution, the process can happen rapidly. Modern bones that fall into mineral springs can become permineralized within a matter of weeks." (Philip J. Currie & Eva B. Koppelhus, *101 Questions about Dinosaurs*, Dover Publications, Mineola, New York, p. 11, 1996)

- Fast fossil formation

- Radiometric dating methods

"The understanding of radioactivity allowed physicists to explain how the Sun and Earth's cores could still be hot after millions of years. In this way, it removed the last scientific objection to what many geologists and paleontologists thought was the great age of the Earth and the Sun. After this, Christians and Jews either had to give up belief in the literal truth of the Bible or resign themselves to intellectual irrelevance." (Steven Weinberg, "Four Golden Lessons," *Nature* 426, p. 389, 2003)

"In general, dates in the correct ballpark are assumed to be correct and are published, but those in disagreement with other data are seldom published, nor are the discrepancies fully explained." (Richard L. Mauger [Assoc. Prof. of Geology, East Carolina University, USA], "K-Ar Ages of Biotites from Tuffs in Eocene Rocks of the Green River, Washakie, and Uinta Basins, Utah, Wyoming, and Colorado," *Contributions to Geology, University of Wyoming* 15(1):37, 1977)

- Assumptions behind dating methods

    Original ratio of elements is known

    Rate of decay is constant

    No addition/subtraction of elements

- The RATE project

- Why people reject the idea of a global Flood

"Then, as now, men often perceive what they expect, and overlook what they do not wish to see." (Colin A. Russell, "The Conflict Metaphor and Its Social Origins," *Science and Christian Belief* 1(1):25, 1989)

Video Review Questions

1. Read Genesis 7 and 9:8-17. What do these passages indicate about the extent of the Flood?

2. In light of the teaching that Noah's Flood covered the whole earth, let's return to the question we asked at the beginning of this lesson: Where was the Garden of Eden located?

3. How does an acceptance of "millions of years" of earth history destroy the global nature of the Flood?

4. Why do you think people reject the idea of a global flood rather than believing the biblical account? How will you respond to such individuals in the future?

5. List some geologic formations that you are familiar with. In each case, what were you taught about when and how it formed? Since watching the video, how have your ideas changed about the ages and processes?

6. Let's apply the biblical understanding of geology to Devils Tower in Wyoming, USA. Hand out copies of the Devils Tower *Wonders of Geology* brochure (available online at www.AnswersIn Genesis.org/ devils_tower).

Arguments Creationists Should NOT Use

When sharing with those who don't believe the Bible, make sure your arguments are up-to-date. Faulty arguments can ruin the credibility of creationists. (For this reason, it is important to stay current by reading sound creationist literature.)

Following is an argument that some people have used to confirm that dinosaur-like creatures were alive until recently. This claim is now out of date and should no longer be used.

For a more extensive list of arguments creationists should not use, see www.AnswersInGenesis.org/dont_use.

- **"The Japanese trawler *Zuiyo Maru* caught a dead plesiosaur near New Zealand."** This carcass was almost certainly a rotting basking shark, since their gills and jaws rot rapidly and fall off, leaving the typical small "neck" with the head. This has been shown by similar specimens washed up on beaches. Also, detailed anatomical and biochemical studies of the *Zuiyo Maru* carcass show that it could not have been a plesiosaur.

DID YOU KNOW?

There are multitudes of examples of geologic processes happening quickly, rather than over many thousands or millions of years as is commonly thought:

1. In 1952, several army planes crash-landed in Greenland. Less than forty years later, in 1988, the planes were found ... under 250 feet of ice! Find out more at www.AnswersInGenesis.org/squadron.

2. Wood has been petrified in a lab in a matter of days! See www.AnswersInGenesis.org/wood.

3. Depth-sounding measurements have shown that coral reefs can grow 414 millimeters per year. At such a rate, the largest coral reef in the world (the Eniwetok Atoll in the Marshall Islands) could have formed in less than 3,500 years! See www.AnswersIn Genesis.org/coral.

4. A canyon, 1/40th the scale of Grand Canyon, was formed in one afternoon by mudflows from Mount St. Helens! See www.AnswersInGenesis.org/helens.

People to Know

STEVE AUSTIN

Steve Austin earned his PhD in geology from Pennsylvania State University. His professional memberships include the Geological Society of America, the American Association of Petroleum Geologists, the Society for Sedimentary Geology and the International Association of Sedimentologists. He is currently a professor with the Institute for Creation Research and has focused his research on Grand Canyon and Mt. St. Helens.

ANDREW SNELLING

Andrew A. Snelling, BSc (Hons), PhD (Geology), was for many years a geologist, senior research scientist and editor of *TJ* at *Answers in Genesis* in Australia. He now works for *Answers in Genesis–US* where he is the Director of Research and editor-in-chief for *Answers Research Journal*.

STEVEN WEINBERG

Dr. Weinberg is a Professor of Physics at the University of Texas at Austin and a Nobel laureate.

Life Application

Let's consider how we can apply the things we've learned today to our lives.

1. Using the same news items from last week, evaluate the reports and determine when radiometric dating methods have been used to yield an age for a fossil or rock formation. As you read the articles, how does what you've been learning affect your understanding of what is being reported?

2. When you hear reports that identify local geological events with Noah's Flood, how will you respond?

For Next Week

For the next lesson, please read and meditate on these verses as part of your preparation:

- Genesis 1:1
- Genesis 1:15–19
- Nehemiah 9:5–6
- Job 9:7–9
- Psalm 8:1–4; 33:6; 102:24–26; 136:1–9
- Isaiah 42:5
- Jeremiah 32:17
- Colossians 1:16

Optional Activities

(These will be assigned at your teacher's discretion.)

1. Choose a landform (coal, caves, Grand Canyon, Yellowstone, etc.) that interests you. After researching it, write a paper on how you think it formed, from a biblical perspective (for some ideas, see www.AnswersInGenesis.org/geology).

2. Research different processes that you've been told "prove" the earth is old. Write a paper summarizing your findings.

Glossary of Terms

The following term is discussed in this lesson:

ARTICULATED

Arranged in a connected sequence, such as bones of a skeleton that remain in the same arrangement they were when the animal was alive.

BIG PROBLEMS
WITH THE BIG BANG

Video Notes

- Overview of the big bang

- Biblical problems with the big bang
    Cause of the universe

    Timescale

    Order of events

    Future

    E.T.

    Original earth

- Basis of science fiction

- Review of the issue of death and suffering before Adam's sin

- Two different versions of history

- Who do you trust?

- Definition of a scientific model

- Scientific problems with the big bang
  Flatness

  Horizon

  Singularity

  Baryon number

Distant mature galaxies

Population III stars

• Why do people believe the big bang?

Video Review Questions

1. Briefly describe, in your own words, the big bang concept. After watching the video, how have your views about the big bang changed?

2. What do the following verses teach about the origin of the universe? Genesis 1:1, 15–19; Nehemiah 9:5–6; Job 9:7–9; Psalm 8:1–4; 33:6; 102:24–26; 136:1–9; Isaiah 42:5; Jeremiah 32:17; Colossians 1:16.

3. Of all the *biblical* problems with the big bang, which one stands out the most to you? Why?

4. Of the *scientific* problems with the big bang, which one stands out the most to you? Why?

5. What new insights have you gained about how the Bible relates to astronomy?

6. What is the definition of a scientific model? How will remembering this definition help you to evaluate models that you may read about?

7. Despite all the scientific problems with the big bang theory, why do so many people continue to believe it?

8. Why do you think some Christians believe in the big bang idea?

Arguments Creationists Should NOT Use

In the past, some creationists advocated a geocentric view of the solar system, claiming that it is taught by the Bible. However, as the following paragraph explains, this is a false idea that no reputable creationists teach.

For a list of other arguments creationists should avoid, see www.AnswersInGenesis.org/dont_use.

DID YOU KNOW?

1. The man behind the Apollo moon mission was the creationist rocket scientist Wernher von Braun. Another creationist, Jules Poirier, designed some vital navigational equipment used in the space program.

2. At least four different naturalistic explanations have been proposed for the formation of our moon. However, each has its own set of problems. The best explanation for the origin of the moon is that God created it to give light on the earth at night, as Genesis teaches. See www.AnswersInGenesis.org/moon for additional information.

3. Solar astronomer John Eddy has commented about our sun, "I suspect ... that the sun is 4.5 billion years old. However, given some new and unexpected results to the contrary, and some time for some frantic recalculations and theoretical readjustment, I suspect that we could live with Bishop Ussher's value for the age of the earth and sun [about 6,000 years]. I don't think there is much in the way of observational evidence to conflict with that" (Eddy, J.A., quoted by Kazmann, R.G., It's about time: 4.5 billion years, *Geotimes* **23**:18–20, 1978. See www.AnswersInGenesis.org/sun for additional information about the sun.)

- **"Geocentrism (in the classical sense of taking the earth as an absolute reference frame) is taught by Scripture, so heliocentrism is anti-scriptural."** AiG rejects geocentrism and believes that the biblical passages about sunset, etc., should be understood as taking the earth as a reference frame, one of many physically valid reference frames; the center of mass of the solar system is also a valid reference frame. See www.AnswersInGenesis.org/geocentricism for additional information.

People to Know

COPERNICUS (1473–1543)

In the sixteenth century, Copernicus postulated that the earth and planets revolve around the sun. See www.AnswersInGenesis.org/galileo for additional information.

JOHANNES KEPLER (1571–1630)

The most significant scientific advance in the field of planetary motion was made by the German astronomer and mathematician Johannes Kepler. For more information, see www.AnswersInGenesis.org/kepler.

ISAAC NEWTON (1642–1727)

Isaac Newton is well known as one of the greatest scientists who ever lived. Less well known is his deep belief in God and his conviction that scientific investigation leads to a greater knowledge of God, the Creator of the universe. See www.AnswersInGenesis.org/newton for additional information.

Life Application

Let's consider how we can apply the things we've learned today to our lives.

The big bang story is taught all around us—in museums, planetariums, textbooks, news articles. Knowing what you know about the biblical and scientific problems with the big bang, how will you respond when confronted with this false idea? Do you know anyone who accepts the big bang explanation of the origin of the universe? Discuss some ways to talk to those who accept this idea.

For Next Week

Please read and meditate on these verses in preparation for the next lesson:

- Acts 17:11
- Deuteronomy 10:14
- Deuteronomy 11:17
- 1 Chronicles 29:10–12
- Psalm 19:1–6
- Psalm 89:11–12, 148
- 2 Peter 3:10–12

Optional Activities

(These will be assigned at your teacher's discretion.)

1. Research additional problems with the big bang, such as a particular problem that Dr. Lisle mentioned. Write a research paper explaining them.

2. Research how can we see light from stars millions of light-years away in a universe that is 6,000 years old? Write a paper reporting your findings.

3. Research the life and work of Kepler, Newton or Copernicus. Write a paper summarizing your research.

Glossary of Terms

The following terms are discussed in this lesson:

EPICYCLES

In Ptolemaic cosmology, a small circle, the center of which moves on the circumference of a larger circle at whose center is the earth and the circumference of which describes the orbit of one of the planets around the earth.

GEOCENTRIC

The idea that the sun and other planets revolve around the earth.

HELIOCENTRIC VIEW

The view that the planets revolve around the sun.

KELVIN / ABSOLUTE ZERO

A temperature scale in which zero occurs at absolute zero and each degree equals one kelvin. Water freezes at 273.15 K and boils at 373.15 K.

MODEL

A schematic description of a system, theory or phenomenon that accounts for its known or inferred properties and may be used for further study of its characteristics.

A good model is relatively simple (the fewer assumptions, the better the model) and makes many correct, specific predictions.

MONOPOLE

Particles which have either a north or south magnetic pole, but not both.

SINGULARITY

The condition in which the universe was supposedly all together in a single point.

ASTRONOMY
What Do We Really Know?

Video Notes

- Two big mistakes

- Beliefs have consequences

- Maintain integrity

- Criteria for distinguishing truth from fiction:
    Biblical

    Operational

Origins

Incorrect criterion

Peer review

Video Review Questions

1. Describe, in your own words, the criteria we should use to help distinguish truth from fiction.

2. What principle, discussed today, is found in Acts 17:11? Besides the big bang, in what other ways can you apply this principle in your life?

3. Let's return to the question we asked before the video. How have your ideas about astronomy changed, based on what you saw in the video?

4. Fill out the disciplines chart. Take a few minutes to think about which aspects of astronomy fall under operational science and which fall under origins science.

DISCIPLINE: ASTRONOMY	OPERATIONAL SCIENCE	ORIGINS SCIENCE

5. What do the following verses teach about God and the heavens? Deuteronomy 10:14; 11:17; 1 Chronicles 29:10–12; Psalm 19:1–6; 89:11–12; 148; 2 Peter 3:10–12.

6. Why is it not necessary that truth agree with our intuition?

DID YOU KNOW?

When *Voyager 2* flew by Uranus in 1986, making many images and measurements, evolutionists received a shock. "To the complete astonishment of scientists, the magnetic axis [of Uranus] is tilted approximately 60 degrees with respect to its axis of rotation. It is not known why." The strength of the magnetic field was also a surprise to evolutionists, but not to creationists. Creationist astrophysicist Dr. Russell Humphreys, using biblical assumptions, had accurately predicted the strength two years previously! See www. AnswersInGenesis.org/uranus.

Arguments Creationists Should NOT Use

The following arguments should be avoided as evidence for a young universe:

- **"Moon dust thickness proves a young moon."** For a long time, creationists claimed that the dust layer on the moon was too thin if dust had truly been falling on it for billions of years. They based this claim on early estimates—by evolutionists—of the influx of moon dust, which caused worries that the moon landers would sink into this dust layer. These early estimates were wrong, and by the time of the Apollo landings, NASA was not worried about sinking. So the dust layer thickness can't be used as proof of a young moon (or of an old one, either). See www.AnswersInGenesis.org/moondust for additional information.

- **"The gospel is in the stars."** This is an interesting idea, but quite speculative, and many biblical creationists doubt that it is taught in Scripture, so we do not recommend using it.

People to Know

MICHAEL OARD

Michael J. Oard has a masters of science degree in atmospheric science from the University of Washington. He worked as a meteorologist/weather forecaster for the US National Weather Service, and he published several papers in his field in widely recognized journals.

Life Application

Let's consider how we can apply the things we've learned today to our lives.

Many aspects of astronomy (including the big bang) are often mentioned as fact, rather than just human ideas about the origin and workings of the universe. Examine the articles your teacher gives you. Take some time to analyze what the articles are reporting. Which statements are facts and which are interpretations?

For Next Week

Please read and meditate on these verses in preparation for the next lesson:

- Genesis 1:1–31
- Matthew 19:4–6

Optional Activities

(These will be assigned at your teacher's discretion.)

1. Research the various astronomical evidences that confirm the biblical account of a universe that is 6,000 years old. Write a report summarizing your findings.

2. Research the lives and work of present-day creation astronomers (see www.AnswersInGenesis.org/bios for help). What degrees have they earned? Where did they study? What professions have they chosen? What types of careers are available to Christians in the field of astronomy or astrophysics?

3. Write a paper on "The Heavens Declare the Glory of God."

Glossary of Terms

The following terms are discussed in this lesson:

CANDLE

Basic unit of luminous intensity adopted under the Systeme International d'Unites; equal to 1/60 of the luminous intensity per square centimeter of a black body radiating at the temperature of 2046 K.

DARK MATTER

Dark matter is material which emits little or no light/radiation (and therefore cannot be seen) but is detected by its gravitational influence on other (visible) objects.

OPERATIONAL (OBSERVATIONAL) SCIENCE

Science that deals with repeatable, observable processes in the present.

ORIGINS (HISTORICAL) SCIENCE

Science that deals with past events—unique, unrepeatable, unobservable events.

PARALLAX

An apparent change in the direction of an object, caused by a change in the observer's position that provides a new line of sight.

10

A NEW REFORMATION PART 1
Changing Lives, Rocking the Culture

Video Notes

- Finding the answers to the gay marriage and abortion issues—without the Bible?

"Let me make one caution to those of you who are going to be carrying this fight forward through our neighborhoods and through our civic associations and through our communities and through our churches—and eventually to the halls of political power in America ... .

The Bible is all truth, it is God's truth, it is revealed propositional truth without error. But you can't argue from that when you're arguing the question of marriage in society ... . You have to argue on grounds of justice and prudence. ... What is a just society? That's a question people have asked since the time of the Greeks ... .

I would say that anyone looking at what's just for society says we've got to first do what is best due for those kids. So, make the argument with your secular neighbors and with politicians on the basis of what is good and just and right for society as a whole." (**Prominent evangelical Christian leader in the United States**)

- Jesus, Genesis and the gay marriage issue

- Destroying the doctrines of Christianity

- Why doesn't society listen to the Bible?

- The Church in England—what's happened?

- George Barna research

- Why do we see increasing gay marriages, removal of Ten Commandments, abortions, divorces, racism, etc.?

- Satan's tactics in the garden and today

- Millions of years—where do you fit them into the Bible?

"It is apparent that the most straightforward understanding of the Genesis record, *without regard to all of the hermeneutical considerations suggested by science*, is that God created heaven and earth in six solar days, that man was created in the sixth day, that death and chaos entered, the world after the Fall of Adam and Eve ... " (Pattle P.T. Pun, "A Theology of Progressive Creationism")

"We have to admit here that the exegetical basis of the creationists is strong ... . In spite of the careful biblical and scientific research that has accumulated in support of the creationists' view, there are problems that make the theory wrong to most (including many evangelical) scientists ... . Data from various disciplines point to a very old earth and an even older universe ... ." (Dr. James Boice [pastor and speaker on the Bible Study Hour], *Genesis: An Expositional Commentary,* vol. 1, pp. 57–62)

"From a superficial reading of Genesis 1, the impression would seem to be that the entire creative process took place in six twenty–four–hour days. If this was the true intent of the Hebrew author ... , this seems to run counter to modern scientific research, which indicates that the planet Earth was created several billion years ago ... ." (Gleason L. Archer [Old Testament scholar], *A Survey of Old Testament Introduction*)

"The question concerning the age of the earth comes down to a matter of interpretation, both of science and the Bible ... .

"Biblically, we find the young earth approach of six consecutive 24–hour days and a catastrophic universal flood to make the most sense. However, we find the evidence from science for a great age for the universe and the earth to be nearly overwhelming ... . Therefore, we believe we must approach this question with humility and tolerance for those with different convictions." (Rich Milne and Ray Bohlin, *Christian Views of Science and Earth History*)

- Compromise positions on Genesis 1

    Gap theory

    Theistic evolution

    Progressive creationism

    Day-age theory

    Framework hypothesis

- The Bible's history—if it's not true, then one doesn't have to believe the Bible's doctrines, morality or the gospel because they are based in that history.

Video Review Questions

1. Did Jesus address the "gay marriage" issue? If so, what did He say about it?

2. If someone wanted to remove the doctrines of Christianity from a place in society, what would be the best way to go about it?

3. Why isn't the abortion issue being won in our society?

4. Why is America becoming less Christian every day? (Hint: Ken's 11:3 talk)

5. Explain how Satan attacks the authority of the Word of God today in the same way that he did with Eve in the garden.

6. Which much-repeated word in Genesis 1 do people want to re-define because of the influence of evolutionary ideas and belief in long history over millions of years?

7. Explain where millions of years were squeezed into the Bible when theologians first accepted the geologists' idea of an old earth.

8. Why don't many Christian leaders believe in six literal 24-hour days and a young earth?

9. What is a person really saying when he or she believes God used evolution or the big bang?

10. What do all compromise positions of the Bible have in common?

11. What did church leaders in England give up that caused Christianity to crumble in that country?

People to Know

CHARLES HADDON SPURGEON (1834–1892)

Although he never attended a seminary, Spurgeon was England's best-known preacher in the second half of the nineteenth century. He frequently preached to audiences exceeding 10,000. He also founded Sunday schools, churches, an orphanage and the Pastor's College. He edited a monthly church magazine and promoted literature distribution. His printed works are voluminous.

JOHN WESLEY (1703–1791)

Anglican clergyman, evangelist and founder of Methodism. He graduated from Oxford University and became a priest in the Church of England in 1728.

GEORGE WHITFIELD (1714–1770)

Though a clergyman of the Church of England, he cooperated with and had a profound impact on people and churches of many traditions. Along with the Wesleys, he inspired revival and evangelism on both sides of the Atlantic. In his preaching ministry, he became known as the "apostle of the British empire."

Life Application

In an effort to connect the Bible to geology, astronomy, biology, etc., what are some steps that Sunday school classes and youth groups could take to teach these subjects in a creative way?

Think about an area that interests you (geology, for example),

and consider how you might share the biblical view of this subject to other inquirers, both believers and nonbelievers.

For Next Week

Please read and meditate on these verses in preparation for the next lesson:

- Psalm 11:3
- Judges 21:25
- Genesis 1:20–21, 24, 29; 2:7; 3:15, 21; 9:3
- John 10:9

Optional Activity

(These will be assigned at your teacher's discretion.)

Find examples in the Bible or in recent media reports that show Satan creating doubt in the minds of believers. Think about times in your own life when you've experienced Satan using this tactic on you. Write down the examples and discuss them with the group.

Glossary of Terms

The following terms are discussed in this lesson:

DAY-AGE THEORY

The idea that the creation days in Genesis 1 were not literal, 24-hour days, but were long ages of time.

EXEGETICAL

An extensive and critical interpretation of any text, especially of Holy Scripture.

FRAMEWORK HYPOTHESIS

This theory asserts that Genesis 1 is not to be taken as a literal, chronological account of creation, but rather as a topical account which asserts that God created all things.

GAP THEORY

The belief that there is a gap in time between Genesis 1:1 and Genesis 1:2. The classic gap theory teaches that the geological ages took place over billions of years of earth history. At the end of these geological ages, a great cataclysm took place on earth. Then God recreated the earth in the six literal days of creation as recorded in the first chapter of Genesis.

HERMENEUTICAL

Of or pertaining to interpretation. The art of expounding the Scriptures.

PROGRESSIVE CREATION

This theory, as popularized by astronomer Hugh Ross, allows millions of years to be added to the Bible. The theory teaches that the universe was a result of the big bang, which occurred 16 billion years ago, that the days of creation were vast ages, that the sun and stars were created before the earth, that God created almost all species separately, that animals were eating each other for millions of years before mankind existed, that Noah's Flood was just a local event and that the seventh day of Creation Week is still continuing.

THEISTIC EVOLUTION

The idea that God, over long periods of time, used evolutionary processes to bring about all physical life forms from a single organism.

YOM

Yom is the Hebrew word for "day." This word can have many meanings—a period of daylight, time, a specific point in time, a year, or a period of 24 hours. Its meaning depends on the context—the words surrounding *yom.*

Throughout the Old Testament, when the phrase "evening and morning" or a number (such as "first") is used with *yom,* it refers to a period of 24 hours—a normal–length day, not "time" in general or a "year" or "millions of years."

A New Reformation Part 2
Changing Lives, Rocking the Culture

Video Notes

- Bible's history and the message of Jesus Christ

- Psalm 11:3—"If the foundations be destroyed what can the righteous do?"

- Book of Judges and today's culture

- One of the most-asked questions in the world

- Death, bloodshed and disease among humans and animals

- The saddest day in history

- After Noah's Flood, things changed

- After the Fall, God withdrew some of His sustaining power

- The Bible explains why we wear clothes

- Jesus Christ stepped into history to serve a mission

- What a beautiful world it is—not really

- Blaming God and believing in death before sin

- Big picture of death

- The message of Grand Canyon is "repent"

Video Review Questions

1. What book of the Bible includes a story that is similar to what we see in our society today, where few people believe in moral absolutes?

2. What was the original diet of animals and mankind? When did God give people permission to eat meat?

3. Explain why, biblically, plants are not considered "alive."

4. Explain what happened on the saddest day in the history of the universe.

5. Read Genesis 3. Describe some of the results of Adam's sin. What other things have resulted from the curse that God pronounced in Genesis 3?

6. What is the biblical explanation for wearing clothes?

7. Where in the Bible is the first mention of the gospel?

8. Explain the naturalistic view of death. How does this view of death affect a person's view of God?

9. After tragedies, such as earthquakes or tsunamis that kill thousands of people, how should a Christian respond to the question, "How could a loving God let all those innocent people die?"

10. Explain the underlying message of Grand Canyon.

11. Explain how Noah's Ark is a "type" of Jesus Christ.

DID YOU KNOW?

The late Charles Templeton, former well-known evangelist who was once listed among those "best used of God" by the National Association of Evangelicals, rejected Christianity based on his view of death. He described his slide into unbelief in his book *Farewell to God*, in which he listed several "reasons for rejecting the Christian faith." They include the following:

- Geneticists say it is "nonsense" to believe that sin is the "reason for all the crime, poverty, suffering, and general wickedness in the world."

- The "grim and inescapable reality" is that "*all life is predicated on death*. Every carnivorous creature *must* kill and devour another creature. It has no option."

Templeton had a big problem understanding how to reconcile the loving God of the Bible with an earth full of death, disease and suffering. Templeton stated:

> Why does God's grand design require creatures with teeth designed to crush spines or rend flesh, claws fashioned to seize and tear, venom to paralyze, mouths to suck blood, coils to constrict and smother—even expandable jaws so that prey may be swallowed whole and alive? ... Nature is, in Tennyson's vivid phrase, "red [with blood] in tooth and claw," and life is a carnival of blood.

Templeton then concludes: "How could a loving and omnipotent God create such horrors as we have been contemplating?"

See www.AnswersInGenesis.org/slide for additional information.

Life Application

Let's consider how we can apply the things we've learned today to our lives.

Think of some things you could do to help educate others about the biblical view of death.

For Next Week

Please read and meditate on these two chapters in preparation for the next lesson:

- Genesis 3
- Romans 8

Optional Activities

(These will be assigned at your teacher's discretion.)

1. Find articles (both secular and Christian) that deal with tragic events, and compare how these articles treat death.

2. Explain the big picture of these deaths from God's perspective.

Glossary of Terms

The following terms are discussed in this lesson:

ENMITY

Hatred

NEPHESH

A Hebrew word which conveys the basic idea "breathing creature." People and animals are described in Genesis as having, or being, *nephesh*. See Genesis 1:20–21, 24, where *nephesh chayyah* is translated "living creatures," and Genesis 2:7, where Adam became a "living soul" (*nephesh chayyah*). Plants do not have *nephesh*, so Adam's eating of a carrot did not involve death in the biblical sense.

12

A New Reformation Part 3
Changing Lives, Rocking the Culture

Video Notes

- Not dealing with the sin of one generation

- The "age of the earth" stumbling block

"If God is omnipotent and omniscient, why didn't he start the universe out in the first place so it would come out the way that he wants? Why is he constantly repairing and complaining? No, there's one thing the Bible makes clear: The biblical God is a sloppy manufacturer. He's not good at design, he's not good at execution. He'd be out of business if there was any competition." (Carl Sagan, *Contact*, Pocket Books, New York, p. 285, 1985)

"Whatever the God implied by evolutionary theory and the data of natural history may be like, He is not the Protestant God of waste not, want not. He is also not a loving God who cares about His productions. He is not even the awful God portrayed in the book of Job. The God of the Galapagos is careless, wasteful, indifferent, almost diabolical. He is certainly not the sort of God to whom anyone would be inclined to pray." (David L. Hull, "The God of the Galapagos," *Nature* 352:486, Aug. 8, 1992)

- God pronounced His original creation "very good"

"To adopt the explanation of design, we are forced to attribute a host of flaws and imperfections to the designer ... . We would also have to attribute every plague, pestilence, and parasite to the intentional actions of our master designer. Not exactly a legacy calculated to inspire love and reverence ... . Finally, whatever one's view of such a designer's motivation, there is one conclusion that drops cleanly out of the data. He was incompetent." (Kenneth R. Miller [Roman Catholic, cell biologist, professor of biology at Brown University, coauthor of widely used high school and college biology textbooks], *Finding Darwin's God*, Cliff Street Books, pp. 101–102, 1999)

- Charles Darwin and the "death" issue

"Annie's cruel death destroyed Charles' tatters of beliefs in a moral, just universe. Later he would say that this period chimed the final death-knell for his Christianity. St. Charles now took his stand as an unbeliever." (A. Desmond and J. Moore, *Darwin: The Life of a Tormented Evolutionist*, W.W. Norton & Company, New York, p. 387, 1991)

- Consequences of having a wrong view of history

"Turner is a strident nonbeliever, having lost his faith after his sister, Mary Jane, died of a painful disease called systemic lupus erythematosus. 'I was taught that God was love and God was powerful,' Turner said. 'And I couldn't understand how someone so innocent should be made or allowed to suffer so.'" (*Ted Turner Was Suicidal after Breakup, New York Times* web page, April 16, 2001)

"I believe that there is no supreme being with human attributes—no God in the biblical sense—but that life is the result of timeless evolutionary forces, having reached its present transient state over millions of years." (Charles Templeton, *Farewell to God*, McClelland & Stewart, Toronto, p. 232, 1996)

"The grim and inescapable reality that all life is predicated on death. Every carnivorous creature must kill and devour another creature. It has no option." (Charles Templeton, *Farewell to God*, McClelland & Stewart, Toronto, p. 232, 1996)

"Nature is, in Tennyson's vivid phrase, 'red in tooth and claw,' and life is a carnival of blood." (Charles Templeton, *Farewell to God,* McClelland & Stewart, Toronto, p. 199, 1996)

"I believe that, in common with all living creatures, we die and cease to exist as an entity." (Charles Templeton, *Farewell to God,* McClelland & Stewart, Toronto, p. 233, 1996)

- What doesn't get preached—the Bible's history

- Today's social ills are merely symptoms of a greater problem

- Genesis: a side issue?

- The solution—a new Reformation

Video Review Questions

1. In England 40–50% of the population once attended church. Today, the church is dying, and some experts estimate that the church in England will be dead and buried in 40 years. Why?

2. What happens when the sins of one generation aren't dealt with? How does this relate to the age of the earth?

3. Explain how the age of the earth can be a stumbling block to someone hearing and accepting the gospel of Jesus Christ.

4. Explain the misleading picture painted by sugary hymns like "All Things Bright and Beautiful."

5. How has an acceptance of "millions of years" undermined biblical authority and driven generations away from the church?

6. Explain how unbelief has been sweeping across the United States and the once-Christian West.

7. Explain what is meant by the statement, "The removal of the 10 began with an attack on the 6."

8. What is Ken referring to when he mentions "Christian Patriot missiles"?

9. What are some things that need to happen for revival to sweep our culture?

People to Know

MARTYN LLOYD–JONES (1899–1981)

Widely acclaimed as Britain's greatest preacher of the twentieth century. Under his leadership, Westminster Chapel of London was established as the foremost evangelical pulpit in England.

MARTIN LUTHER (1483–1546)

German theologian, professor and pastor who began the Protestant Reformation with the posting of his Ninety-Five Theses (on October 31, 1517) on the door of the Castle Church in Wittenberg. This triggered the movement in world history known as the Reformation, the rediscovery of the unvarnished gospel, the good news of salvation by grace through faith in Jesus Christ.

Life Application

Let's consider how we can apply the things we've learned today to our lives.

What things can you do to become like a Martin Luther within your sphere of influence? Write down some things you could do to help bring people back to biblical authority or to show new believers that the Bible's history is true.

Optional Activities

(These will be assigned at your teacher's discretion.)

1. Conduct research and write a short paper on the life of Martin Luther during the Reformation.

2. Look at different commentaries in various Bibles and see how the writers have interpreted (and reinterpreted) Genesis 1–11.

Glossary of Terms

The following terms are discussed in this lesson:

ESCHATOLOGY

The branch of theology that is concerned with "end times."

SOLA SCRIPTURA

A Latin phrase meaning "Scripture alone." It is one of the most central Protestant beliefs to come out of the Reformation. This Protestant doctrine says that Scripture alone is the primary and absolute source of authority.

QUESTIONS & ANSWERS

Video Notes

- Genesis

- Geology

- Astronomy

- Miscellaneous

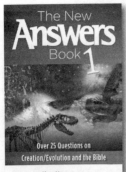
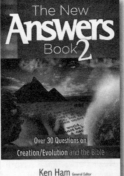
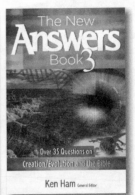

Ultimate Apologetics DVD SET

Dr. Jason Lisle

In this 4-DVD boxed set, astrophysicist Dr. Jason Lisle explains how to defend biblical creation in a way that is absolutely irrefutable. Unlike so much literature on origins, this series deals with the heart of the issue, showing that the Bible is the bottom line. The Bible must indeed be what it claims: the authoritative Word of God. Otherwise the gospel message itself—of original sin and the need for Jesus Christ—is without foundation. *Approx. 58 minutes each. (Ages 15 and up)*

The Ultimate Proof of Creation BOOK

Dr. Jason Lisle

Tens of thousands of readers have discovered a defense for creation that is powerful, conclusive, and has no true rebuttal. As such, it is an irrefutable argument—an "ultimate proof" of the Christian worldview. Dr. Lisle shows that engaging an unbeliever, even a staunch atheist, is not difficult when you use the proven techniques described here. 254 pages. (Jr. High–Adult)

Already Gone

Ken Ham & Britt Beemer

Reveals startling facts discovered through scientific surveys of a thousand 20–29 year olds who used to attend church regularly. The results are shocking! There is a huge disconnect between the questions children are asking and what our churches are teaching. 192 pages. (Jr. High–Adult)

Audiobook 3 hours, 46 minutes. (Jr. High–Adult)

The Lie

Ken Ham

Ken Ham is best known for his message on the relevance of creation and the importance of Genesis. Humorous and easy to read, this book powerfully equips Christians to defend the book of Genesis and opens eyes to the evil effects of evolution on today's society. 168 pages. (Junior High–Adult)

Search for the Truth

Bruce A. Malone

Over 100 one-page "articles" that explain the evidence for creation and the relevance of creation to modern society. Articles are laid out so that they can be reprinted in local newspapers, church bulletins, Sunday school lessons, homeschool supplements, or as witnessing tools. Copiously illustrated, including cartoons by the renowned Chuck Asay. 144 pages. (Jr. High–Adult)

Me, the Professor, Fuzzy, and the Meaning of Life

Follow the author and illustrator, David Pensgard, on this graphic journey of logic that culminates in the wonderful conclusion that God is a logical deduction, and Christianity is the only rational truth. An excellent and nonthreatening witnessing tool for teens and young adults. 216 pages. (Jr High–Adult)

Call 1-800-778-3390
or visit www.AnswersBookstore.com